ABDO Publishing Company

BUGS!
Beetles

Kristin Petrie

visit us at
www.abdopublishing.com

Published by ABDO Publishing Company, 8000 West 78th Street, Edina, Minnesota 55439.
Copyright © 2009 by Abdo Consulting Group, Inc. International copyrights reserved in all
countries. No part of this book may be reproduced in any form without written permission from the
publisher. The Checkerboard Library™ is a trademark and logo of ABDO Publishing Company.

Printed in the United States.

Cover Photo: Peter Ambruzs/CritterZone.com
Interior Photos: Alamy pp. 16, 25; Andy Williams/CritterZone.com pp. 24, 27; AP Images p. 28;
    David Cappaert/Bugwood.org p. 19; Getty Images p. 17; iStockphoto pp. 7, 10, 12, 19, 22, 23,
    29; National Geographic Image Collection p. 5; Peter Ambruzs/CritterZone.com pp. 1, 8, 11;
    Peter Arnold pp. 9, 13, 19, 20, 21; Photo Researchers p. 15

Series Coordinator: BreAnn Rumsch
Editors: Megan M. Gunderson, BreAnn Rumsch
Art Direction & Cover Design: Neil Klinepier

Library of Congress Cataloging-in-Publication Data

Petrie, Kristin, 1970-
  Beetles / Kristin Petrie.
      p. cm. -- (Bugs!)
  Includes index.
  ISBN 978-1-60453-063-6
  1. Beetles--Juvenile literature. I. Title.

  QL576.2.P48 2008
  595.76--dc22

                         2008004776

Contents

Brilliant Beetles

What do the ladybug, the potato bug, and the **dung** bug all have in common? They do not look alike, nor do they eat the same things. Yet, all of these bugs are beetles! Beetles are the world's most common type of insect.

Entomologists believe there are more beetle species than any other type of animal species. In fact, they estimate that there are millions of beetle species on Earth. Of these, only 350,000 species are known. Yet, more species are discovered every year. One thing is for sure. Millions of beetle species means trillions of individual beetles!

Beetles come in many shapes, sizes, and colors. And, they have different features to meet their individual survival needs. For example, plant-hoppers have long legs. Nut-eaters have sharp jaws, and water-lovers have an oxygen tank.

Many beetle species are beautiful to look at. Some are shiny, brightly colored, or just unusually shaped. The most beautiful beetles are known as jewel beetles.

These variations make beetles a **diverse** group of insects. In fact, many people don't know a beetle when they see one. But keep reading, and you will begin to recognize many bugs for what they are. Beetles!

What Are They?

Beetles are insects. Like all insects, they belong to the class Insecta. Within this class, beetles belong to the order Coleoptera. The known species in this order make up about 40 percent of all known insect species. This makes Coleoptera the largest order in the animal kingdom.

That's a lot of beetles! How do **entomologists** decide which bugs are actually beetles? The beetle's wings are an important factor. Beetles are different from other insects because of their hard, thick wings.

The order Coleoptera is divided into four **suborders**. These suborders are further divided into about 170 families. Some of these families include rove beetles, leaf beetles, scarab beetles, and click beetles.

Each species of beetle has a two-word name called a binomial. A binomial combines the genus with a descriptive name, or epithet. For example, a seven-spotted ladybug's binomial is *Coccinella septempunctata*.

The rhinoceros beetle can grow up to 7 inches (18 cm) long. It is recognized for the hornlike structures on its head.

This longhorn beetle has unusual coloring. Will you recognize the next beetle you see?

THAT'S CLASSIFIED!

Scientists use a method called scientific classification to sort the world's living organisms into groups. Eight groups make up the basic classification system. In descending order, they are domain, kingdom, phylum, class, order, family, genus, and species.

The phrase "Dear King Philip, come out for goodness' sake!" may help you remember this order. The first letter of each word is a clue for each group.

Domain is the most basic group. Species is the most specific group. Members of a species share common characteristics. Yet, they are different from all other living things in at least one way.

Body Parts

Like all insects, beetles have six legs, three body **segments**, and no bones. Instead of bones, insects have a stiff outer coating called an exoskeleton. It protects the insect's **organs**.

A beetle's exoskeleton splits into two sections down the center of its back. These sections form hard wings called elytra. The elytra have two jobs. They protect the beetle's insides and its second pair of wings.

Most people recognize the hard shell of a beetle's back. But few realize that underneath is a soft and sometimes hairy body!

The second set of wings is for flight. These hind wings are thin and delicate, with veins running through them. When not in use, the hind wings fold and collapse under the elytra. The combination of elytra and hind wings is **unique** to the beetle order of insects.

When in flight, elytra and large hind wings make a
beetle look much larger than it actually is.

A beetle's three body **segments** are the head, the thorax, and the abdomen. Like many insects, a beetle's head is small when compared to its other body segments.

On its head, a beetle has bulging compound eyes. Compound eyes have many lenses connected as one. They allow the beetle to see colors and motion well.

The beetle's chewing mouthparts are called mandibles. The shape and size of the mouth and jaws vary depending on the beetle's diet. A beetle that eats soft plants and insects has small jaws for cutting leaves or crushing seeds. A predatory beetle has strong, sharp jaws for stabbing or crushing prey.

Fan-shaped antennae

Saw-toothed antennae

Big or small, beetles are well known for biting. In fact, the term beetle *comes from words meaning "little biter."*

A beetle's head also sprouts feelers, or antennae. Antennae are very important. They allow beetles to sense the world around them. A beetle uses its antennae to smell food, choose a mate, and find its way home.

Antennae usually have 11 **segments**, but they vary in form. Beetle feelers can be long and tube shaped, saw-toothed, or fan shaped. These shapes depend on a beetle's **environment**, diet, and other factors.

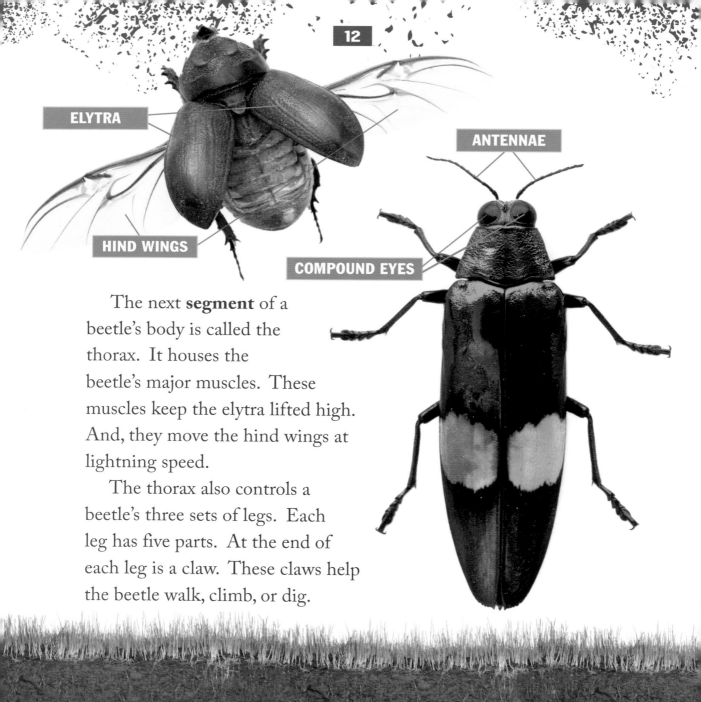

ELYTRA

ANTENNAE

HIND WINGS

COMPOUND EYES

The next **segment** of a beetle's body is called the thorax. It houses the beetle's major muscles. These muscles keep the elytra lifted high. And, they move the hind wings at lightning speed.

The thorax also controls a beetle's three sets of legs. Each leg has five parts. At the end of each leg is a claw. These claws help the beetle walk, climb, or dig.

Beetle legs may be short or long, furry or bare. These features depend on the function of the legs. For example, a beetle that jumps from leaf to leaf needs long legs for leaping. A beetle that lives underground needs short, strong legs for digging.

A beetle's last body **segment** is the abdomen. The abdomen is the largest of the three segments. That is because it houses many of the beetle's **organs**.

A BEETLE'S BODY

HEAD

THORAX

ABDOMEN

MANDIBLES

LEGS

The Inside Story

Inside a beetle, several **organs** and systems function together to keep its body moving. These systems help the beetle breathe, **digest** food, and survive in a variety of places.

A beetle's respiratory system is not like a human's. Did you know that a beetle does not have lungs? Instead, it obtains oxygen through small holes in its abdomen. These holes are called spiracles. Tubes called tracheae connect to the spiracles. They carry oxygen throughout the beetle's body.

Beetles have a circulatory system called an open system. This means the beetle's blood flows freely through its body. Beetle blood is called hemolymph. The heart is a long tube that runs the length of the beetle's body. It moves the hemolymph from end to end.

A beetle's nervous system consists of a simple brain and a **nerve** cord. The brain is made of clusters of nerves, or ganglia. The nerve cord connects the brain to ganglia in the thorax and the abdomen. Nerves extend from the cord through the beetle's body. These nerves help the beetle function.

Thanks to their body systems, beetles have adapted and survived for thousands of years.

Transformation

Fireflies aren't the only light-producing insects. But, they are the only insects that can flash their lights in distinct signals.

A beetle takes on several forms during its lifetime. Beetles go through complete **metamorphosis**, which has four stages. They are egg, larva, pupa, and adult. However, beetles must mate before this life cycle begins.

Not surprisingly, beetles have many different mating **rituals**. For instance, male firefly beetles attract mates with patterns of light signals. Other beetles tap out messages with their heads. Most beetles send chemicals called **pheromones** into the air to attract a mate. The scent of the pheromones indicates that a beetle is ready for mating.

After mating, males of most species do not help females raise their young.

After mating, the female must find a safe nest. The ideal place to lay eggs is protected and near food. When the female lays the **fertilized** eggs, growth begins. This is the first step in **metamorphosis**.

Once the eggs are deposited, most beetle species leave them to grow on their own. But, some beetles stay with the nest to guard their young from predators.

The larval stage is the second step in metamorphosis. Larvae often look like squirmy worms. Why are they so wiggly? Larvae are very hungry! They eat nonstop to fuel their growth.

This rapid growth requires a larva to **molt** many times. Each time it sheds its skin, a new, larger skin forms. Depending on the species, the larval stage can last from a few weeks to several years!

After the larvae's growth is complete, they enter the pupal stage. Pupae are much less active than larvae. Their growth spurt is over, but their transformation is not. During this stage, a pupa molts for the last time. Finally, it becomes an adult beetle.

BUG BYTES

June bug larvae live underground for two years. They head toward the surface during heavy spring rains. Then around the month of June, they appear aboveground by the thousands.

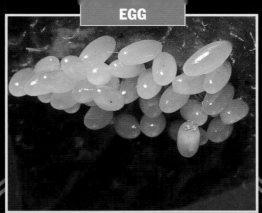

EGG

LIFE CYCLE OF A BEETLE

LARVA

ADULT

PUPA

Beetle Homes

Where do beetles live? Everywhere! The only places you will not find beetles are in the ocean and at the North and South poles. Great numbers of beetles are found in warm, wet regions. However, they can also be found in the middle of the desert!

How can beetles keep from frying in the middle of a desert? What allows them to live in a pond or a stream? Why don't they freeze in the snowy mountains? Beetles have an amazing ability to adapt to their surroundings.

Desert beetles dig deep into the cool ground to avoid the heat. Water beetles have an oxygen pocket under their wings for long dives. Cold-weather beetles make their homes in plant tissues or belowground to stay warm. Or they move to someone else's warm home, like yours!

Some desert beetles have white elytra. The color helps them stay cool by reflecting the sun's heat.

Giant diving beetles are well adapted to life in the water. Their hind legs are covered in hairs that act like paddles. This helps them swim swiftly.

Most humans don't like to share their homes with bugs. But many other creatures don't mind at all. For example, certain ant species let beetles live in their nests. The beetle keeps the place clean by eating the ant **colony**'s waste. In exchange, the beetle gets to live in an **environment** that is safe from predators.

Some beetles make their home right on another animal, or host. Often, the host is already decaying. These beetles lay their eggs on the carcass, which their larvae will feed on. Other beetles live in the fur of live hosts.

Another beetle home you might find gross is near the droppings of certain animals. It's true! Some beetles make their home in a pasture or a nest. This way they can be close to **dung**, their favorite food.

Stag beetles live for three to five years as larvae, feeding on rotting wood. When they emerge as adults, they live only from May until August. Some scientists believe that no food is eaten during this time.

Probably the best place to find less disgusting beetles is in your backyard or at a park. Simply turn over a rock, peer into a rotted tree, or dig under a pile of dead leaves. These are ideal homes for beetles. Why? They don't have to leave home to eat!

Dung beetles lay their eggs in dung balls. The larvae eat the dung after they hatch.

AN ANCIENT SYMBOL

ANCIENT EGYPTIANS REGARDED ONE TYPE OF DUNG BEETLE AS SACRED. TO THEM, THE SCARAB SYMBOLIZED THEIR SUN GODS. THESE GODS ROLLED THE SUN ACROSS THE SKY EACH DAY AND BURIED IT EACH NIGHT. THE EGYPTIANS BELIEVED THIS ACTION WAS REPRESENTED IN THE SCARAB'S HABIT OF ROLLING AND BURYING DUNG BALLS.

SO, COINS AND JEWELRY WERE MADE WITH IMAGES OF SCARABS. WEALTHY EGYPTIANS WORE THIS SYMBOL OF GOOD LUCK ON THEIR CLOTHING. EVEN MUMMIES WERE BURIED WITH SCARAB ORNAMENTS OVER THEIR HEARTS. TODAY, THE SCARAB IS A WELL-RECOGNIZED SYMBOL OF THE ANCIENT EGYPTIANS.

Delicious Dishes

Weevils do not have chewing mouthparts. Instead, they use their snout to pierce and suck. So, they are sometimes called snout beetles.

You've learned about some of the interesting food choices beetles make. **Dung**, dead animals, and rotten wood are favorites for some beetles. However, less revolting food selections are more common.

Weevils feed on many plant parts. These beetles eat roots, stems, leaves, and fruit. Each weevil species picks a specific plant part to feed on. The rest of the plant is left for other insects to snack on.

Predatory beetles hunt other living creatures. For example, soldier beetles feed on soft insects such as aphids. And certain ground beetles are sneaky hunters. At night, they climb plants and

BUG BYTES

Museums sometimes use dermestid beetles to clean up the bones used in exhibits. These flesh-eating larvae can remove all traces of soft tissue from a skeleton in no time!

find sleeping insects to eat. Drowsy caterpillars make an easy, tasty meal.

After a beetle chews, food passes into the gizzard. This tubelike **organ** is lined with teeth that grind up the food for **digestion**. **Nutrients** are then absorbed into the beetle's body for energy and growth.

Beware!

Yes, beetles prey on innocent insects. But other insects eat beetles, too! Beetles are an important part of the food chain. They fill the stomachs of birds, snakes, frogs, and other animals. They must also watch out for spiders, ants, and other beetles.

Despite the dangers around them, beetles survive. Beetles are good little fighters! Their methods of defense are impressive and sometimes amusing. For example, some beetles use their sharp jaws to bite and wrestle. Others spurt poisonous liquids at their enemies. Still other beetles give off a stinky smell or a bad taste. Predators learn the hard way to leave these beetles alone.

The most common methods used to avoid danger are running and hiding. Some beetles have long legs and can move quickly. Other lucky beetles blend right into the scenery. Predators never even see them. And of course, another effective way to get overlooked is to play dead!

BUG BYTES

A water beetle called the whirligig beetle has an extra pair of eyes on the underside of its head. This allows the beetle to watch above and below the water's surface at the same time.

Darkling beetles, or stinkbugs, are sometimes called clown beetles. This is because they do a "headstand" when threatened. Then, they squirt a bad-smelling substance from their rear end.

TOUGH TRICKSTERS

CLICK BEETLES HAVE A SPECIAL WAY OF PROTECTING THEMSELVES FROM ENEMIES. MOST BEETLES CANNOT RIGHT THEMSELVES IF THEY ARE FLIPPED ONTO THEIR BACKS. HOWEVER, CLICK BEETLES HAVE A HOOKLIKE PART ON THE UNDERSIDE OF THEIR BODIES. BY BUILDING UP PRESSURE IN THE THORAX AND THEN RELEASING THE HOOK, THESE BEETLES JERK THEIR BODIES UPRIGHT. THIS ACTION PRODUCES A LOUD CLICKING NOISE THAT CAN SCARE OFF PREDATORS.

THE BLISTER BEETLE GETS ITS NAME FROM THE DAMAGE IT CAN DO. WHEN IN DANGER, THIS DARK BEETLE OOZES AN OILY LIQUID FROM ITS LEG JOINTS. ONE TOUCH, AND YOU OR ANY OTHER PREDATOR HAS SEVERELY BLISTERED SKIN.

Beetles and You

Most beetles are harmless. Yet some are pests. Carpet beetles eat carpet and wooden furniture. Japanese beetles kill fruit trees, corn crops, and many flowering plants. Colorado potato beetles can destroy entire potato fields.

On the other hand, beetles have been used to control other damaging insects. For example, farmers appreciate ladybugs. These beetles feast on aphids, which eat many types of crops. In fact, farmers have been known to buy ladybugs to protect their fields.

Other beetles are important to the **environment**. They are vital to the breakdown of plant and animal matter. Without these creepy recyclers, we would have a world covered with dead stuff!

Fortunately, most beetles simply coexist with us and nature. If you really

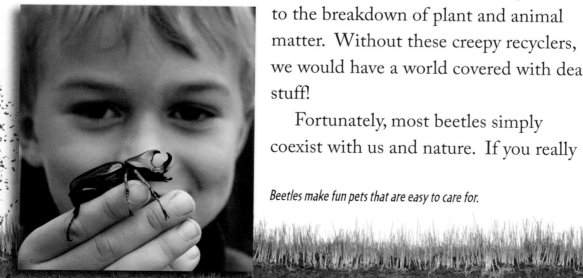

Beetles make fun pets that are easy to care for.

Ladybugs are scary predators to aphids, scales, and mealybugs.
One ladybug larva can eat between 50 and 200 aphids per day!

like beetles, you can catch them for closer inspection. Even if you are grossed out, you can still admire them from a distance. Either way, you have some fascinating facts to think about the next time you see a beetle.

Glossary

colony - a population of plants or animals in a certain place that belongs to a single species.

digest - to break down food into substances small enough for the body to absorb. The process of digesting food is called digestion.

diverse - composed of several distinct pieces or qualities.

dung - animal waste.

entomologist - a scientist who studies insects.

environment - all the surroundings that affect the growth and well-being of a living thing.

fertilize - to make fertile. Something that is fertile is capable of growing or developing.

metamorphosis - the process of change in the form and habits of some animals during development from an immature stage to an adult stage.

molt - to shed old skin and replace it with new skin.

nerve - one of the stringy bands of nervous tissue that carries signals from the brain to other organs.

nutrient - a substance found in food and used in the body to promote growth, maintenance, and repair.

organ - a part of an animal or a plant that is composed of several kinds of tissues and that performs a specific function. The heart, liver, gallbladder, and intestines are organs of an animal.

pheromone - a chemical substance produced by an animal. It serves as a signal to other individuals of the same species to engage in some kind of behavior.

ritual - a form or an order to a ceremony or an event.

segment - any of the parts into which a thing is divided or naturally separates.

suborder - a group of related organisms ranking between an order and a family.
unique - being the only one of its kind.

How Do You Say That?

antennae - an-TEH-nee
Coleoptera - koh-lee-AHP-tuh-ruh
elytra - EHL-ih-truh
entomologist - ehn-tuh-MAH-luh-jihst
ganglia - GANG-glee-uh
hemolymph - HEE-muh-lihmf
larvae - LAHR-vee
metamorphosis - meh-tuh-MAWR-fuh-suhs
pheromone - FEHR-uh-mohn
pupae - PYOO-pee
tracheae - TRAY-kee-ee

Web Sites

To learn more about beetles, visit ABDO Publishing Company on the World Wide Web at **www.abdopublishing.com**. Web sites about beetles are featured on our Book Links page. These links are routinely monitored and updated to provide the most current information available.

Index